IMPERFECT LOVE

IMPERFECT
LOVE

Poems
by
MILLER WILLIAMS

Louisiana State University Press
Baton Rouge and London
1986

Copyright © 1983, 1984, 1985, 1986 by Miller Williams
All rights reserved
Manufactured in the United States of America

Designer: Christopher Wilcox
Typeface: Palatino
Typesetter: G&S Typesetters, Inc.
Printer: Thomson-Shore, Inc.
Binder: John Dekker & Sons, Inc.

Library of Congress Cataloging-in-Publication Data
Williams, Miller.
  Imperfect love.
  I. Title.
PS3545.I5335215   1986   811'.54   86-7399
ISBN 0-8071-1357-3
ISBN 0-8071-1358-1 (pbk.)

Some of the poems included here have appeared in the following publications: *America, American Poetry Review, Georgia Review, Negative Capability, Southern Review,* and *Yankee.*

"One Day a Woman," "One of Those Rare Occurrences on a City Bus," "Mecanic on Duty at All Times," "Stopping to Look at a Crèche in a Jewelry Store Window," and "A Summer Afternoon an Old Man Gives Some Thought to the Central Questions" originally appeared in *The Kenyon Review.*

"A Poem for Emily," "The Aging Actress Sees Herself a Starlet on The Late Show," "Tearing Down the Hotel," and "On a Trailways Bus a Man Who Holds His Head Strangely Speaks to the Seat Beside Him" originally appeared in *Poetry.*

"*In extremis* in Hardy, Arkansas" is reprinted from *New England Review and Bread Loaf Quarterly,* Vol. IX, No. 1 (September, 1986).

Sam Houston is the originator of the remark about dogs and loyalty used as his own by the boss in "The Promotion."

Thank you, Jean.
Thank you, Martha.
Thank you, Mary.

for Jordan

CONTENTS

One Day a Woman 1
One of Those Rare Occurrences on a City Bus 2
WW I 3
Divorce 4
Mecanic on Duty at All Times 5
Recognition 6
And Also Much Cattle 7
The Law and The Prophet 8
Jonathan Aging 9
Politics 10
After a Brubeck Concert 11
My Wife Reads the Paper at Breakfast
   on the Birthday of the Scottish Poet 12
Despairing of Understanding We Fall into Decadence 13
On a Photograph of My Mother at Seventeen 14
The Vanishing Point 15
For Lucinda, Robert, and Karyn 16
A Poem for Emily 17
Staying 18
Animals 19
Entropy 20
On Seeing Projected Figures
   for War Dead in the 20th Century 21
A Little Poem 22
The Vondarc 23
After the Funeral for a Young Woman
   Who Played Her Guitar on the Corner 24
In a Motel Room
   After Coming upon a Car Wreck 25
Why People Feel Lonely at Odd Times 26
When I Am Dead, My Dearest 27
The End Is Here. Nuke Russia. 28
Stopping to Look at a Crèche in a Jewelry Store
   Window 29
The Truth at the Heart of Geometry 30
Mark 5:1–17; One of the Crowd on the Shore
   Tells How It Was 31

Tearing Down the Hotel   32
The Promotion   33
A Summer Afternoon an Old Man Gives Some
    Thought to the Central Questions   35
The Aging Actress Sees Herself a Starlet on the Late
    Show   37
Schumann Adds Trombones to His Second Symphony
    After Mendelssohn Conducts the First Performance   38
The Senator Explains a Vote   39
In extremis in Hardy, Arkansas   42
Love in the Cathedral   44
On a Trailways Bus a Man Who Holds His Head Strangely
    Speaks to the Seat Beside Him   46
Ruby Tells All   48
After the Revolution for Jesus
    a Secular Man Prepares His Final Remarks   50

IMPERFECT LOVE

ONE DAY A WOMAN

One day a woman picking peaches in Georgia
lost her hold on the earth and began to rise.
She grabbed limbs but leaves stripped off in her hands.
Some children saw her before she disappeared
into the white cloud, her limbs thrashing.
The children were disbelieved. The disappearance
was filed away with those of other women
who fell into bad hands and were soon forgotten.
Six months later a half-naked man in Kansas
working on the roof of the Methodist Church
was seen by half a dozen well-known
and highly respected citizens to move
directly upward, his tarbrush waving,
until he shrank away to a point and vanished.
Nobody who knew about the first event
knew of the second, so no connection was made.
The tarbrush fell to earth somewhere in Missouri
unnoticed among a herd of Guernsey cows.

ONE OF THOSE RARE OCCURRENCES
ON A CITY BUS

For exactly sixty seconds riding to work
approaching a traffic light going to green
he understands everything. I mean from the outer
curling edge of the universe to quarks,
the white geometries of time, of language,
death and God, the potted plants of love.
He sits there and looks at the truth. He laughs.
What could we want, except for him to laugh?
Understanding all, he understands
he has only sixty seconds, then he returns
to live with us in ignorance again,
and little enough to laugh at. "Do you have a pen,"
he says to the man beside him,
"that I could use?" The man pats his pockets
and shakes his head and shows his open palms
to say that he is sorry. Fifty-three. Fifty-four.

WW I

Even tomorrow he may leave his room
to get the *Times* out of the holly bush
and there before him see a battleground:
trenches, the mud, the rats, the bombs that bloom
so small a man could die alone in one,
Mademoiselle from Armenteers, the sound
of tiny planes made of canvas and tin.
He may look at his watch or check the sun;
he may wait for orders to move on out,
or once more get the *Times* and take it in.

DIVORCE

A man existed for seventeen spidery years
in the crawl space under the rafters of his home.

His Ford was found on a bridge.
His wife stood on the slick riverbank
shifting from foot to foot
as if she had gone there with the wrong congregation.

That was when he slipped into the house.

He came down by night and took some food.
Only enough so nobody would notice.

In two or three years he learned to tell by sound
like a blind man what happened in the rooms beneath him.

He heard the children grow up as the music changed.
The girl was a Brownie Scout for a little while
and then the phone began to ring all day.
The boy let the screen door slam till he graduated.

Sometimes his wife would bring a man home.
He understood everything,
the shutting of the door,
the stumbling in the dark,
the quietness that occupied the house.

MECANIC ON DUTY AT ALL TIMES

The license plate was another state and year.
The man's slow hands, as if they had no part
in whatever happened here, followed the hollows
and hills of his broad belt. Inside the car
four children, his face again, with eyes like washers,
were as still as the woman, two fingers touching her cheek.
"How much?" he said. "Well maybe fifty dollars
if I can find a used one. I guess I can."
The hands paid no attention. Out in the sun
light wires dipped and rose and dipped again
until they disappeared. *Flats fixed* and *Gas*
and *Quaker State* squeaked in the wind. Just that.
And the speeding trucks, wailing through their tires.

RECOGNITION

A customer saw one time in a flower shop
another man he thought he recognized.
The man turned around and the customer saw
his own sweet eyes looking calmly toward him,
not in the least surprised, clearly aware
of something going on in the flower shop.

AND ALSO MUCH CATTLE

> Conversing with himself
> the young country preacher
> stays true to his faith

A man tells a woman that he was blind
from birth and lately found a medical chance
to see and took it.
This is a lie he tells to be in her pants.

He says he has therefore the eyes of a child,
not having seen a woman naked. He knows
what she will do.
She is going to take off all her clothes.

And then will he be blind in hell? He will.
But will it matter when he's all afire?
Then blind the child.
The child did neither pleasure nor conspire.

Guilt follows the flesh. The books of good and evil
will all fall out of balance if God forgets.
No matter to Him
how hard you pray, God, please, He collects His debts.

True love has little use for sentiment,
and time, if you live forever, must seem odd.
He probably tries
to see things as we do. How can He, being God?

THE LAW AND THE PROPHET

He scorns the flesh and tithes and prays a heap
and celebrates the suffering God imposes,
with little Love or Faith, in trembling Hope
that dark will not come down when the long door closes.

JONATHAN AGING

Jonathan feels like a character out of Dickens.
He's served foods he can't digest anymore.
He feels things move that never have moved before.
His graying hair grows thin and his body thickens.

He thinks of mortality more than he used to.
He knows his wife has seen that his arms are soft,
that he has neither time nor interest left
to do the things she still wants to do.

He finds time for another glass of scotch
before dinner, is still surprised to hold
the paper so far away and misread his watch.

If it confuses him how people grow old
to curse the lapsing of the heart and crotch,
it was never a secret and he was certainly told.

POLITICS

Mowing the lawn, having done with a tangle
of briar, with yellow jackets in the eaves,
he is imposing order, but he leaves
some ragged grass where fences make an angle,
trapping a small shadow most of the day.
There, in the swarming morning, circling twice,
his dog turns herself intently clockwise
then drops on the flattened grass. In this way
she reshapes the world to suit a hound.
A square yard of his yard he leaves to her
because he sees that both of them are bound
as Jesus, Jefferson, and Caesar were
(as all people are, and some small friends)
to change a stubborn world to fit their ends.

AFTER A BRUBECK CONCERT

Six hundred years ago, more or less,
something more than eight million couples
coupled to have me here at last, at last.
Had not each fondling, fighting, or fumbling pair
conjoined at the exquisitely right time,
thirty-four million times, I would be an unborn,
one of the quiet ones who are less than air.
But I will be also, when six hundred years have passed,
one of seventeen million who made love
aiming without aiming to at one
barely imaginable, who may then be doing
something no one I know has ever done
or thought of doing, on some distant world
we did not know about when we were here.
Or maybe sitting in a room like this,
eating a cheese sandwich and drinking beer,
a small lamp not quite taking the room from the dark,
with someone sitting nearby, humming something
while two dogs, one far away, answer bark for bark.

MY WIFE READS THE PAPER AT BREAKFAST ON THE BIRTHDAY OF THE SCOTTISH POET

Poet Burns to Be Honored, the headline read.
She put it down. "They found you out," she said.

DESPAIRING OF UNDERSTANDING
WE FALL INTO DECADENCE

All of our innocence does not console us
for what we don't know. Sometimes, even so,
there is pleasure in spite of our ignorance.

We lie on the living room rug like empty lizards.
With dinner candles and one lamp burning
we read all night, Wyatt and Homer and Keats,

who taught us the love of earth and of what stumbles on it,
of time, even, and change, the breath of time,
and death, and the flickering possibility.

Down its long descent of nights and days
the tumbling earth turns us toward the sun
and sends us sleepy to bed, out of phase

with the first stirring birds and yawning beasts
and billions of imperceptibly shifting leaves.
We rouse ourselves past ten, with no chores done.

ON A PHOTOGRAPH OF
MY MOTHER AT SEVENTEEN

How come to town she was, tied bright and prim,
with not a thought of me nor much of him.

Now, tied to a chair, she tries to pull free
of it and the world. Little is left of me,

I think, or him, inside her teetering head
where we lie with the half-remembered dead.

Her bones could be as hollow as a bird's,
they are so light. Otherness of words.

They could be kite sticks. She could be a kite;
that's how thin her skin is. But now some light

from somewhere in the brain comes dimly through
then flickers and goes out. Or it seems to.

Maybe a door opened, where other men
and women come and go, and closed again.

How much we need the metaphors we make
to say and still not say, for pity's sake.

THE VANISHING POINT

Often I squinted my courage to see the spot
where all lines converge, but only saw
my father before it, spreading like a tree.

He is diminished now into that unplace
where there is nothing, neither breath nor breadth,
and I have felt a generation move.

I am standing, it seems all of a sudden,
with no one now between that point and me,
sliding toward it slowly as I can.

I grieve to celebrate. And may my children,
back down the widening years, see before them
some such old and serviceable simile.

FOR LUCINDA, ROBERT, AND KARYN

I leave you these, good daughters and honest son,
to have or toss away
when all is said and done:

a name that rocks like a boat; some thoughts begun;
a fondness for instruments I didn't play.
I leave you these, fair daughters and far son:

a sense of the probable (the one
sure anchor for the brain); a place to stay
as long as it stands. When all is said and done

you'll share the glory I won, or might have won,
for things I said or things I meant to say.
I leave you these, tough daughters and rocky son:

a tick no springs or brain or batteries run;
the valley in the mattress where I lay.
When all is said and done,

I'll leave my unpaid debts to everyone,
a slow love and resentment's sweet decay.
I'll leave you to yourselves, my daughters, my son,
when what's to say and do has been said and done.

A POEM FOR EMILY

Small fact and fingers and farthest one from me,
a hand's width and two generations away,
in this still present I am fifty-three.
You are not yet a full day.

When I am sixty-three, when you are ten,
and you are neither closer nor as far,
your arms will fill with what you know by then,
the arithmetic and love we do and are.

When I by blood and luck am eighty-six
and you are someplace else and thirty-three
believing in sex and god and politics
with children who look not at all like me,

sometime I know you will have read them this
so they will know I love them and say so
and love their mother. Child, whatever is
is always or never was. Long ago,

a day I watched awhile beside your bed,
I wrote this down, a thing that might be kept
awhile, to tell you what I would have said
when you were who knows what and I was dead
which is I stood and loved you while you slept.

STAYING

What are we to do with this hour of the evening
when the curving distinction between the sky and the sea
is almost gone
and the waves breaking white on the dark shore
and falling back
sound like the steady breathing of some long creature
sleeping or waiting?

In a small house high above the water
smiling for no reason I can name
you pick up a deck of cards and begin to shuffle.
We are both pleased by the riffle of the shuffling cards
which is not like any other sound.

ANIMALS

I think the deaths of domestic animals
mark the sea changes in our lives.
Think how things were, when things were different.
There was an animal then, a dog or a cat,
not the one you have now, another one.
Think when things were different before that.
There was another one then. You had almost forgotten.

ENTROPY

You say Hello and part of what you spend
to say it goes to God. There is a tax
on all our simplest thoughts and common acts.
It will come to pass that friend greets friend
and there is not a sound. Thus God substracts
bit by little bit till in the end
there is nothing at all. Intend. Intend.

ON SEEING PROJECTED FIGURES
FOR WAR DEAD IN THE 20TH CENTURY

No age was less assured a heaven waits
to welcome home the souls it liberates,
or ever so proficient as our own
at freeing them from bondage to the bone.

A LITTLE POEM

for Jack Marr

We say that some are mad. In fact
if we have all the words and we
make madness mean the way they act
then they as all of us can see

are surely mad. And then again
if they have all the words and call
madness something else, well then—
well then, they are not mad at all.

THE VONDARC

This beast, with habitat of indefinite range,
uncertain markings and size, and disputed sound,
either drags its belly on the ground
or flies from tree to tree. Nothing is strange
if not that, when occasionally it feeds,
it eats itself—it is likely alone
in this respect—and passes through its own
digestive tract; less so, that when it breeds
it screws itself. What issue comes, is killed.
It would sit high on each endangered list
except that—having paw and fin and fist,
and being scaled and feathered, lunged and gilled—
it has no place. Some say it looks a lot
like ugly things on cornices in Rome,
though sometimes something very close to home
seems to suggest itself; no one says what.

AFTER THE FUNERAL FOR A YOUNG WOMAN WHO PLAYED HER GUITAR ON THE CORNER

Death is a lie the devil tells

If death's a lie, what is an old guitar,
what is a glass of water, a pair of shoes,
or this, the almost solid stuff we are?

We mow the lawn, we wash the dented car,
we sweep the front porch, we pay our dues.
If death's a lie, what is an old guitar?

We are startled to realize how far
that body goes from wanting light or news
or this, the almost solid stuff we are.

The torn flesh becomes a crooked scar;
the beaten flesh becomes a bright bruise.
If death's a lie, what is an old guitar?

We believe the sun is a special star.
We can trust in any gods we choose
or this, the almost solid stuff we are.

Men have smiled, bathing, to smell a bar
of soap a woman may have smiled to use.
If death's a lie, what is an old guitar?
Or this, the almost solid stuff we are?

IN A MOTEL ROOM
AFTER COMING UPON A CAR WRECK

Looking at someone dead by accident
we say *that could happen to me*
and we pay attention to what we're doing awhile.

But we can stand by beds of people dying
of old age as if the translucent bodies
belonged to another species.

We rarely see ourselves
in those small beds being watched.

It is not because it smells like death
that we turn away from the foul breath.
We are brave enough, taking our chances
with loveliness and dust.

It is because it smells like certainty.

It is not so terrible that one day we may,
but that some unmarked hour we must.

WHY PEOPLE FEEL LONELY AT ODD TIMES

Perhaps before you finish reading this
you will know that something has gone wrong;
perhaps before you pull in air enough
to make a small sound to get the attention
of whoever that is in the other chair
your pores will spill like springs of chilly water,
your feet will be still, forgetting all they knew;
your eyes will open wide, then lose all interest.

The only means of perception we have now
is this person rising from the other chair.

WHEN I AM DEAD, MY DEAREST

Sing what you want to sing. Romanticize.
Let anyone who wants to lie, tell lies.
What will I care, back in the past tense
with no ambition and not a whit of sense,
back where I was until the egg and sperm
began to be something like a worm
that learned to turn, to look sidelong and smile.
I will stay this time an endless while
and will not think that wrong or wish it right
more than a log in darkness hopes for light.
You will say my name, but less with the years,
the children less than you and more than theirs.
It is in our names, as they fray and thin,
blown on the breaths of aging friends and kin,
that sometimes, my dearest, we may seem
to sleep on a little past the dream.

THE END IS HERE. NUKE RUSSIA.

Sign carried by a woman in a white dress on a street in Boston

The end is with us always,
waiting in our cars, on stairs, in hallways,

our bathtubs and our beds.
We hold its ways hidden inside our heads.

The end is small, discrete
and personal as when we wash our feet.

The world each brain commits
comes to its lonely close if the brain quits.

But we have come to mix
statecraft and faith in such a politics

as Mather might have dreamed,
and all is more in common than it seemed.

Mather made smaller fires.
Having fashioned to our own desires

vindictive gods, we may
out of our heads invent a judgment day.

STOPPING TO LOOK AT A CRÈCHE
IN A JEWELRY STORE WINDOW

Burros, taken to Death Valley by prospectors
and lost in the desert, by eating the few grasses
and other green things that grew there, caused the death
of wild goats that lived there and other animals.
But they don't know they did that, being asses.

Or so we've assumed, but seeing them gathered round
the portable manger of Bethlehem, with angelic features,
bowed heads, and bending knees, one has to wonder
what they know of guilt and innocence,
these beasts of burden, these simple, braying creatures.

THE TRUTH AT THE HEART OF GEOMETRY

A circle is not a hexagon or dot
or triangle or pentagram or square.
A circle is a circle. The rest are not.

You should not assign a circle a function
foreign to a circle; don't ever ask
a circle to give someone extreme unction,

however much it looks like a priest.
It wouldn't even know what it was doing;
the family wouldn't care for that in the least.

Not to malign the circle. You can't rely
upon those other shapes to do it, either,
but you would never ask them to try.

MARK 5:1–17; ONE OF THE CROWD ON THE SHORE TELLS HOW IT WAS

"What a wonderful thing has come to pass,"
everyone said. It was some day, all right,
for him set free of demons, and his kin.
All of them were Christians after that.
At first the people cheered and clapped their hands.
"Jesus!" they said. "Did you see what he did?"
Except, of course, the owners of the hogs.
I can tell you they had some things to say,
with two thousand pigs running amok.
"The whole damn business gone, the years of work!
How we gonna feed our wives and kids?
Someone's gonna pay for this, by God.
Who the hell does this man think He is?"
After a while this made the crowd uneasy
and then they got to grumbling, nervouslike.
Finally they told the man to leave
but when His boat was almost out of sight
there were the owners, yelling through their hands,
"What are you gonna do about our pigs?"

TEARING DOWN THE HOTEL

They are tearing down the oldest hotel
in Spring Lake, New Jersey. People sat here
in wicker chairs, reading Henry James,
when women wore long dresses and high shoes
and talked to men in hard straw hats and blazers
of motorcars and Egypt. Out of their sight,
men with large hands and unbreakable words
complained to women who never slept enough.

People came here when men in medicine wagons
sold bottles of dark elixir to women who waited
in small, fictitious towns, in houses with fringes,
rocking upstairs for days, the last drop gone.

Cars and aeroplanes and moving pictures,
adventures of goggles and boots, made here once
a surety as bright as a pale wine
caught by candlelight and nearly as brief.
Then they died, but that was different, too.
They died knowing that love by vulgar love,
barring only the yawn of a God grown bored,
eternal generations would bloom above them.

When the structure someone supposes here
to take the place of this hollow hotel
is pulled apart, say in a hundred years,
someone will say, maybe, thinking of us:
they were like this and that, read such and such;
they talked of these matters in those old chairs;
they never quite believed that we would be here
recalling the dead, pulling their buildings down.

THE PROMOTION

We are not a large concern, although compared
to what the firm was when my uncle chose
to let it run itself, we are not small.
I'm glad you both could come. Let me freshen those.
I do not mean to denigrate my uncle,
whose seed this was. No growth, not a hundredfold,
can match the making of something out of nothing.
I give him his due, but he was losing hold
when I had nothing but hold. His mind and body
both would wander. My first day, I thought
he might outlast another clean shirt.
He would go home at noon, but still he taught
me half of what I know. I never suffered
much of an education. I lived in the hills.
I brought a small embarrassment to my uncle
and then a threat and then a battle of wills.
I knew as much as a dog does about Sunday
but I had an ease in speaking. Anyway,
you can't fall out of a well, so I took chances.
Soon my uncle was staying home all day.
I know you've heard I took this company over
by untoward means. This is purely falsehood.
It took no cunning at all—only some courage
and a sense of the differences in right and good
consistent with a changing situation.
That's a Magritte that seems to have caught your eye.
I hope I haven't bored you. Please help yourselves;
my wife made all of these. Then by and by
I had to let my young cousin go.
His father lived in the past; this one carried
the future around with him. He never believed
much in the present world. And then he married
a scarce-hipped woman. You know the kind of girl
that cooks turnips and peas in the same pot,
the kind that gets entailed in her man's affairs.
The kind of woman yours is clearly not.
You can trust a high-breasted woman.

Small women getting undressed will lay their rings
in patterns and turn their stockings right side out,
but this has no effect on the order of things.
Then there was my son, born to my first wife,
a woman with all the qualities of a hound
except loyalty. When he was grown
he smelled the bread and came scratching around.
I gave him the chance you have to give a son
even though this one, born of his mother, lied
so bad his wife had to call the dog.
I'm not at home with words. Believe I tried.
When I saw he couldn't do the job
I offered him the southwest territory.
He's somewhere selling shoes. His wife left him
with nothing but a note. That's a story
I'll tell you sometime when you care to hear it.
A man needs a woman with no disdain
for what the man is, or he has no center
and spends his time in foolishness and pain.
I need a man with pride in what he is not,
a man with simple habits I can trust,
who wants just barely more than what he's got,
who'll do me in if he can, or wait if he must.
But that's enough. My wife is giving the sign
that I must light the candles and choose the wine.
What is your pleasure?

A SUMMER AFTERNOON
AN OLD MAN GIVES SOME THOUGHT
TO THE CENTRAL QUESTIONS

Grass grows out of every sidewalk crack.
Briars have taken the garden.
The arteries of the old dog harden almost audibly.
The basement door is broken and the mice are back.

So this is how things are: this face
that doesn't belong to anybody,
a lot of things I ought to throw away,
the grass that knew its place.

I overdramatize somewhat. There's nothing bricks,
a hoe, some putty, nails, and luck can't fix.
Almost everything is redeemable.
The dog and I are not.

Time sometimes heals the mind
and the metaphorical heart
but ravages all the while the bones and the hair
and the poor, sad, fleshy part.

But this is something we have understood.
This was part of the deal our parents made
back in the very beginning of the dream.

I picked up a young bird yesterday
that I thought was dead.
I was going to throw it away
then one of the delicate gray lids lifted.
The eye was as large
as if a child had drawn it.
It knew me with total recognition
as a thing that would have its way.

The way a dying man
his leg in a bear trap too long
might hear either a bear or a man
coming toward him
and listen with some interest.

So it is at the end
but who would want to be an old house
who, being hammered on all day,
understood nothing?

THE AGING ACTRESS SEES HERSELF A STARLET ON THE LATE SHOW

For centuries only painters, poets, and sculptors
had to live with what they did as children.
Those who trod the boards—I love that—
said their first stumbling lines into air.
Some do still, but most of us who are known
and loved for being people we are not
have reels and reels of old film unrolling
behind us nearly as far as we can remember.
We drag it everywhere. How would you like
your first time doing something to keep repeating
for everyone to look at all your life?

How would you like someone who used to be you
fifty years ago coming into this room?
How would you like it, never being able
to grow old all together, to have yourself
from different times of your life, running around?

How would you like never being able
to stop moving, always to be somewhere
walking, crying, kissing, slamming a door?
You can feel it, millions of images moving;
no matter how small or disguised, you get tired.
How would you like never being able
completely, really, to die? I love that.

for we are slow and move at our own behest.
On the other side we keep a distance
between ourselves and the creatures. We rarely see this,
but gorillas make us nervous; even dogs do.
Between the sinless flesh and the sinless brain
we look uneasily in both directions
and hope for kind attention when we are dead.

It's hard to know, though, with what hard eyes
history may see us. We say to ourselves
that time will vindicate that one, or that one,
but who knows an hour ahead? All we can do
is make a few decisions and die with them.
History is going where it will.

But this is not what you want to know.

The fact is, the world is being invaded
and there is nothing we can do to stop it.
They will capture every government office,
they will control every church and school,
every position of power in the marketplace.
Everything we have will be theirs,
and there is no way for us to stop them
though every last one of us were Herod.
They are the children who were born last night.

One of the hardest things we have to do
is face the awful fact of the ordinary.
The world is dying. Long live the world.
I see you think I am not addressing the question.

While we browse through the evening paper
the streptococcus spawns generations,
but trees, if they could see us, would see us move
so fast we might be invisible.
We measure time by how much time we take.
Perhaps we should be still for a little while
and let things pass. But that isn't in us.

Anyway, if you can't cast a few
votes of your own, why come here at all,
a place full of people you don't like,
except to get your name in the almanac—
which, I may as well admit, is something.
My mother would have loved to see it there.

Why am I telling you this? I'm very sorry;
the bell you hear means I have a roll call.
Has anyone offered you coffee? Please keep the cups.
They have the insignia of the senate on them.

IN EXTREMIS IN HARDY, ARKANSAS

My client is a scoundrel and a thief,
the prosecutor says. While he was not
arrested for a scoundrel, I admit it.
Now he says he is a liar, too.
Using the language in the strictest sense
a rhetorician, yes, would said he lied,
but what he said he said in self-defense,
and after the fact, long after the fact.
I mean, when he was captured, he denied
he was a thief. But can a man be blamed
for letting the justice system do its job
without his crying, "Warm, cool, warm"?
The point is this: before no onerous act
did this man say, "Moth may corrupt, and rust,
but I will not break in." He never claimed
to be the sort of man that you could trust.
He lied not to get, but to get away.

If you are a Jew or Moslem, you have to say
of course you want to take the eyes and teeth.
We know the hard laws of Abraham
our cousins live by, being out of grace.
But all of us have sinned and fallen short.

You must forgive me. That was out of place.
My head apologizes for my heart.
There are no pulpits in this country's courts
and that is meet and right. So mote it be.

A legend, then, for we can learn from legends:
People once believed a wound would get well
if one could have the blade that made the wound
be blest and polished and put to holy use;
and would, conversely, start to run and smell
if that blade were buried in corruption.
No soldier after battle cleaned his sword,
but stuck it in the dung of cows and pigs.
They might have used the cesspool of a prison

the prosecutor means to send this man to
and so ensure the festering of our wounds.

If you say, as I have watched you say,
my client is hopeless, lost among the lost,
you put yourselves in peril. That is despair.

God knows what made the sad man you see,
but I will not insult you with sentiment.
I may only say, to make a point,
how being scorned and scorning come together
like two ends of a tunnel. Go in at one,
sooner or later you come out at the other.

Patient friends, this man has fallen short.
If that were all that you were charged to know,
we could have gone home long ago.
The prosecutor, who had an easy task
compared to mine, the truth being with him,
has left no doubt of it, and little to ask
of you but mercy. All of us can see
my client is a scoundrel and a thief.
Ah, but my friends, you would let him go free
if you could know the man he meant to be.

LOVE IN THE CATHEDRAL

"... except you ravish me."

In the beginning I couldn't speak to you.
Not because the words wouldn't come;
it was because they might. Not words like love,
blooming where they fall; words like come here.
When once you turned to look straight at me
out of a crowd, I thought I must have let

the sounds inside my head come out, like "let
us all go home." I wouldn't say to you
the wet, small words that moved inside of me.
I have thought that faith and patience would come
to no good end, that you would say, "See here!"
and never say, "Well yes, I think I'd love

to follow you home; to tell the truth, I'd love
to have some wine, then talk awhile, then let
you pleasure me." *Expelled to suffer here,*
John Milton wrote of us. I look at you
and in my mind your awful kinsmen come
around every corner, looking for me.

You once talked about the weather with me
and that was something, but it was not love,
did not resemble love. Love ought to come
in recognizable clothes. One day I let
my plain and earthy self talk to you
most gently, saying plainly, "Please come here,"

but everything went wrong, a bah-bah here,
a bah-bah there. You have bumped into me
by accident, I have bumped into you
on purpose on the street where talk of love
was inappropriate, then I have let
my heart hide in the cold and watched you come

laughing and blind. No matter what may come,
give me this: that all this time I stood here
ignored to death and loved you while you let
every chance go; say your glances at me

suggested almost anything but love;
say I know you cry in bed, poor you.

Believe in love. You know that I am here
to let you loose. Here is my flesh for you
who may abide with me till kingdom come.

RUBY TELLS ALL

When I was told, as Delta children were,
that crops don't grow unless you sweat at night,
I thought that it was my own sweat they meant.
I have never felt as important again
as on those early mornings, waking up,
my body slick, the moon full on the fields.
That was before air conditioning.
Farm girls sleep cool now and wake up dry
but still the cotton overflows the fields.
We lose everything that's grand and foolish;
it all becomes something else. One by one,
butterflies turn into caterpillars
and we grow up, or more or less we do,
and, Lord, we do lie then. We lie so much
truth has a false ring and it's hard to tell.

I wouldn't take crap off anybody
if I just knew that I was getting crap
in time not to take it. I could have won
a small one now and then if I was smarter,
but I've poured coffee here too many years
for men who rolled in in Peterbilts,
and I have gotten into bed with some
if they could talk and seemed to be in pain.

I never asked for anything myself;
giving is more blessed and leaves you free.
There was a man, married and fond of whiskey.
Given the limitations of men, he loved me.
Lord, we laid concern upon our bodies
but then he left. Everything has its time.
We used to dance. He made me feel the way
a human wants to feel and fears to.
He was a slow man and didn't expect.
I would get off work and find him waiting.
We'd have a drink or two and kiss awhile.
Then a bird-loud morning late one April
we woke up naked. We had made a child.

She's grown up now and gone though God knows where.
She ought to write, for I do love her dearly
who raised her carefully and dressed her well.

Everything has its time. For thirty years
I never had a thought about time.
Now, turning through newspapers, I pause
to see if anyone who passed away
was younger than I am. If one was
I feel hollow for a little while
but then it passes. Nothing matters enough
to stay bent down about. You have to see
that some things matter slightly and some don't.
Dying matters a little. So does pain.
So does being old. Men do not.
Men live by negatives, like don't give up,
don't be a coward, don't call me a liar,
don't ever tell me don't. If I could live
two hundred years and had to be a man
I'd take my grave. What's a man but a match,
a little stick to start a fire with?

My daughter knows this, if she's alive.
What could I tell her now, to bring her close,
something she doesn't know, if we met somewhere?
Maybe that I think about her father,
maybe that my fingers hurt at night,
maybe that against appearances
there is love, constancy, and kindness,
that I have dresses I have never worn.

AFTER THE REVOLUTION FOR JESUS
A SECULAR MAN PREPARES
HIS FINAL REMARKS

What the blind lost when radio
gave way to TV,
what the deaf lost when movies
stopped spelling out words and spoke,
was a way back in. Always, this desire
to be inside again, when the doors are closed.

On the other side of the doors
our friends and parents and grandparents
work and eat and read books and make sense and love.

The thought of being disconnected
from history or place can empty the heart;
we are most afraid,
whatever else we fear,
of feeling the memory go, and of exile.
And death, which is both at once.

Still, as our lives
are the inhalations and exhalations of gods
we ought not fear those things we know will come
and ought not hope for what we know will not.
The dogs that waited for soldiers to come home
from Philippi, New Guinea, Pennsylvania,
are all dead now whether or not the men
came back to call them.

There is no constancy but a falling away
with only love as a temporary stay
and not much assurance of that.

The desert religions are founded on sandy ways
to set ourselves free from that endless tumbling downward.
Thus we endow ourselves with gods of purpose,
the purposes of gods, and do their battles.

We are sent to war for money, but we go for God.

Prison is no place for living
but for reliving lives.
I remember a quarrel of students

proving, reproving the world;
a woman taking love
she didn't want, but needed
like a drowning swimmer
thrown a strand of barbed wire
by a kind stranger standing on the shore.

Imperfect love in that imperfect world
seemed elegant and right.
Now the old air that shaped itself to our bodies
will take the forms of others.
They will laugh with this air and pass it through their bodies
but days like ours
they will not come again to this poor planet.

I am reinventing our days together.
A man should be careful with words
at a time like this,
but lies have some attraction over the truth;
there is something in deceitful words
that sounds good to the ear.

The first layer of paint conceals the actor;
the second conceals the paint.

By which sly truth we have come to where we are.

I can hear brief choirs of rifles.
Inside my head
naked women wander toward my bed.
How gently they lie there, loving themselves to sleep.

What do we know that matters that Aeschylus did not know?

I do believe in God, the Mother and Father,
Maker of possibility, distance, and dust,
who may never come to judge or quicken the dead
but does abide. We live out our lives
inside the body of God,
a heretic and breathing universe
that feeds on the falling of sparrows

and the crumbling of nations,
the rusting away of metal
and the rotting of wood.
I will be eaten by God.
There is nothing to fear.
To die, the singers believe, is to go home.
Where should I go, going home? Lord, I am here.